Listen
to
the
Golden
Boomerang
Return

CAConrad

Listen
to
the
Golden
Boomerang
Return

Wave Books

Seattle/New York

Published by Wave Books

www.wavepoetry.com

Wave Books titles are distributed to the trade by

Consortium Book Sales and Distribution

Phone: 800-283-3572 / SAN 631-760X

Library of Congress Cataloging-in-Publication Data

Names: CAConrad, author.

Title: Listen to the golden boomerang return / by CAConrad.

Description: First edition. | Seattle : Wave Books, 2024.

Identifiers: LCCN 2023041550 | ISBN 9798891060012 (hardcover) |
ISBN 9781950268962 (paperback)

Subjects: LCSH: Human-animal communication—Poetry. |
Human ecology—Poetry. | Ecology—Poetry. | LCGFT: Poetry.

Classification: LCC PS3603.O555 L57 2024 | DDC 811/.6—dc23/eng/20230926

LC record available at https://lccn.loc.gov/2023041550

Printed in the United States of America

9 8 7 6 5 4 3 2 1

First Edition

Wave Books 115

transmission
was received
inside the
ritual

Listen
to
the
Golden
Boomerang
Return

our first lightning
strike was convulsive
we felt sad for our
violence after
exterminating
wolves and bison
we do not need a
doctor to say
dance dance
dance before
the song
runs out
learn how
to live so
wilderness
never
becomes
mythology
we put them
in parks to be
wild on purpose
a museum of fur
fangs and hooves

part of
this forest
tastes like
the man
I love
with an
actual number
of nails holding
the bedroom
together
other days
when we died
where we fell
we became
the forest
my car never
intended to be
a meat grinder
another face going
under the waves
we felt awful after
hitting the deer
we made love
and slept with
one of his
antlers
between
us

to
desire
the world
as it is
not as
it was
falling
feather
attaches
to new life
for a moment
when the hammer
approached we thought
is that thing coming this way
we are the fractal
drop to hear
our own
harmonics
in the muffled
underground
hum of seeds

remember
our metal skin
when the planet
first caught fire
it was
years
before we
understood
the awful
thing we
held to our chest
whatever a poem can
send into the future
please send the
breath
we have
been trying
to catch
for as long
as you can
hold it
so glad
you came by
thank you
as always

thumbing through
calendars of the future
till touching
a year out
of reach
me a ghost
you a ghost
another poem
dedicated to the
great vanishing trick
we build
muscles
organs bones
at separate
tables
of our
favorite
restaurant
chewing to
motion
kept to
the tides

we stopped
studying the
night sky for
directions
if someone said
we made it up
planet Earth
isn't real
we would try
to verify try
to be sure
critics
are the
evidence
we do not
trust ourselves
your imagination is
asking for parole
what is your
verdict Warden
try to always
remember the
calendar made
of light our
ancestors
followed to
pass the year

plants
are our
  bridge
  to the
      sun
      listen to the ceasefire
      sunlight touching
      everything
      with us
        when did we
        begin to see
        breathing
        bodies as
      targets
      take our place in the
        great chain of beings
        press my fingers
          to each page
        of the new
        notebook
        I cannot stop
          myself feeling
          for words
          before
            they
          arrive

the hill
appeared
in many dreams
        never sure if
    it was real
    Melville
aimed his
gun at the
Transcendentalists
and named it Bartleby
we can prepare
    our shadows to be
        chewed apart or not
        but the chewing
        will commence
I saw a spider eat a fly
I saw a praying mantis
    eat the spider
    I did not mean
    to see these things
        the spider caught my eye
        then the spider was gone
        into the green body
    we begin to discern
    waning time as
seasons through
our organs

folding
hands clouds
make overhead
call upon drifts of
older thoughts
hold it open
all the way
feel the
strain
no more
backslide of
emotion
how long
we have
waited for
this green
stem to live
with us in
the world
my darling
radiant
future
corpse

our
little
places
within
are not
dungeons
remember
remember
astronomers point
satellites into space
the military points
them down at us
the inverse relationship
between love we offer
and what we give
this on and
off button
is another
opportunity
to believe
there are
only two
choices
this too
must end

90 cents
extra for
supernatural
I never dreamed
talking of
empire's
collapse
would
give
you
such a hard-on
there is
tenderness
in the way you
think the FBI is
spying on you
someone in your
imagination cares
as you undress
in the dark
aware of
the fertilizer we
all become on
the calendar's
shrinking
surface

what would it take to
kill the imagination
it is important to
wonder what
our enemies
are already
thinking
you are
so much
blood I
love you
your force
the force
of blood
we give
our thanks
to the engineer
of this meadow
can you hear how it is
flowing through our
door flooding a
better word
sections of
the day peel
away to our
curative
vigor
we were going to be okay
we just did not know it at the time

don't worry
darkness always
accuses us
of falling on
purpose
you know how
to bulldoze
me back up
these hills
what does
darkness know of
light filling your
navel in the
middle of
the afternoon
we have not
lost our
place
in line
shaking
off the cold
let's get this
garden planted
give our fruit
away to one
another

do not live as
though you are a
footnote to the
mention of
a wiggle
timid
hand
reaching into
morning weather
the beach in
california
feels good
because
america
is no longer
in front of us
stop thinking we
got it wrong
lovers friends and
the few I hope to
never see again
keep converting
oxygen with
one breath
then the
next

he said
breathe like you
read your poems
what the hell
does that mean
then suddenly
I'm breathing it
look at our hands
baked into being
by a fleeting magic
bark with dogs to let
the neighborhood know
you can go to
the address
knock all you want
no one is there now
where the exit signs
are burned out
the preexisting
condition is
not cancer
but the
glass of
polluted
drinking
water

after your
purchase
 nails come
  with small
   sounds lasting
    the duration
    of tapping
    them into
     coffin lids
      after which nothing
      awaits but quiet
      not one sympathy
     card contains
    the word death
    if we set the rack
     on fire we can incinerate
      another lever of control
       sunlight currently
       traveling 9 minutes
       through outer space
      to build our bones
     we repeat sunlight
    ETA is 9 minutes
    and counting

refrigerators
are where
we keep our bodies
before they become
our bodies
spinning inside
routines this
living
provides
we sense
language
travel
on our
constant
breath
open a
friend's
refrigerator to yell
Hello Future Friend
human beings are a
symptom of the
Big Bang
gun
stores
fill with
shoppers
bombs mark
the sky with
our pledge

yellow is
the color of
the world's
favorite star
I am a helio
whore hunting
for the deeper
penetration of light
the man I love
pees a golden
halo above my
snow angel
we sing
keep
living
keep alive
singing for
all lives at risk
always remember
you do not
need to like
our star to be
warmed and fed

would
a church
exist if our
fear of death
did not prevail
retire the invisible
arm reaching in and
out of our attention
a tree
reveals
its pulse
to the
leaning
lovers
was that you
it wasn't me
our names
materialize
on lips of
everyone
we love
a brief
frequency
holding each
syllable
midair

a shotgun above every
door where I grew up
I did not mean to
get her ashes
on my shoes
I will wait
to walk in
the rain
refusing
to exert the
stress of time
everyone envied
everyone's shotgun
behind their backs
our favorite game
when I was a baby
was to throw me
off the roof
then run
downstairs
to catch me
oh how we
laughed

a potato
born by
shovel
I am a
bride of
poetry in
my orange
and purple
gown an
unequalled
extinction
machine
pushing
strollers through
ecosystems of
concrete and plastic
we camel through the journey
with our new playbook for
where plunging hands go
don't be weird
about this
you can be a
bride of
poetry
too

never never never never never
said the king at the end
why five nevers
Shakespeare
never said
open for another
all-nighter antennae twitch
you let your queer ass shine
my favorite shine
dilate spirit
our way
blood in
snow in
scene 9
is ketchup
it made us
hungry for
snow we wanted
snow snow snow
on one dinner plate
with two spoons
with extra spicy
tomato blood

battle cry
connects
bodies at
a critical
moment
while love
reveals the
art of pliability
before and after
never so visceral
sing happy
birthday while
harvesting organs
sing happy birthday
while stitching them
into their new body
learn to accept the
unanticipated
wonder for
your hand
when the
moon
reaches
back

do not
solve life
experience it
solidarity with all
targets in motion
paper doll in a pretty
new paper dress
barking paper barks at
the grave beneath
this poem
fluctuating
with american
gunpowder
sales
restless solids
turning liquid
touching our
Hollywood
villains we
thought we
needed
just morbid enough
to bore ourselves

Do You Like
Your Species
is my latest
questionnaire
meet me at the
quarry where
Michelangelo
conjured David
falling is
felt all
over the
body the
next day
imagine
trees hurting
on the forest floor
our every cell
singing the
Ghost of
We Shall
Rise Again
if you call this planet
evil one more time
I will have to learn
to hold you better

if the
marketing
birds do
for love
were
the
only
ad of
the day
do you
puke when
attempting to resist
the violence money costs
going over the freedoms
one at a time
questions
roll in blue
and red
answers
return
home
amethyst

he shows
me how I am
all over his life
alliance of perverts
warms the spot
our butterfly
of inertia
plunging
to the
bottom
of a last
spoonful
with the celebrated
violence of real estate
consciousness
has never been
human alone
we materialize
from behind
the curtain
got to push to shimmer
give more than we take
keep saying it till we do
give more than we take

we
go to
the roof
where stars
are waiting
all my friends hate you
you're like my mean old
tomcat Thor who
alienated us both
from everyone
a most divisive
cat
but I am loyal
all the way
all the
fucking
way my dear
loving you is
holding a piano
note in my head
before shooting
the apple off the
place where my
dreaming gets
done
love
you a lot though

who
stood
outside
arms open
for you to
crash your life into
lowering fork tines
fingering the list of
regrets nailed inside
sentences converge in
the middle of a thought
reporter's recycled
weather map shows
advancing soldiers
rising temperature next to
civilian death toll
we open our bags
find cannonballs
did we shoot these
did we forget the
death we caused

a storm of
handwriting
was this
poem's
first
shape
all that
matters
is which
decisions
today lead me
closer to you
do not fall
away one
two three
a paperboy
delivering his
father's obituary
a footnote to stumbling
in the dark as an art form
come sing
with me into
this dough
what song shall
we bake into
our supper

what was
the point
of today
nothing
more than
microscopic
creatures on
my eyelids
reaching for
sunlight with me
how hard is your
historical memory
as in gay
bashing 101
same day you
learn hieroglyph
means sacred carving
elegy is not a form
it is a state of being the
poet must write from
a faggot takes a beating
from another holy book
and the band said
this is my four-leaf clover
what did they say
this is my four-leaf clover

of course
we look like
punching bags
they only
learned
to punch
a season
known in
the organs
wilt alongside
vase of flowers
go limp just get
dead inside
if I could
see you
again
would
I speak
without
sobbing or
spit curses at
rushing news van
aimed at catastrophe

just
one good
win in the
casino of
america
you must know
what to wear to
a beating for
a softer
fist
after my
boyfriend's
rape and
murder
I stopped
dancing
started
eating
until I was
carrying the
weight of him
everywhere
dragging one
beautiful day
into darkness
after the other
carry it on find the
footing to carry it on

the angel
of death was
created on the first day
introducing everyone
to the temporary
kingdom
poet
cockroach
of the art world
we find our
own level
push our
faces into
orbits we
never
imagined
our poems
notifying the
tormentors
they are working
together now the lovers
you don't
stand a
chance

a quest
to italicize
a period does
not need anyone's
approval any more
than it requires
rude comments
about wasting time
in the middle of our
2nd plague they said
look over here new toys on Mars
looking elsewhere
is another kind
of looking away
it was the same
during the early
years of AIDS
just ask straight
people my age
how can we point at a horizon
yet still fear death
just relax it's not a
white flag out the
window it's my
new panties
I will never
surrender

not nostalgic
for 80s music
I'm reminded of
helping friends
overcome
limits of
hospital
walls
each new
diagnosis
loosened
mortar
between us
dance to George
Michael's Faith
with absolute
determination
just hearing it
exhausts me
I continue
to live to
make Jesus
regret dying
for my sins

a
lion
meddling
with mechanics
of my throat
hooks in
hooks out
eyes write
heart writes
liver writes
liver writes a
little more
then I lift
the pen
prepare
for their
answers
when
speaking
with
the
dead
listen to
the golden
boomerang return

queers will
not die lonely for
you witch-burning
christians of america
I conjure a loving spirit above
the scorched city in my chest
my dear man let's forget their
heterosexual violence for one day
I will describe beautiful flesh you cannot see
back of your neck
shoulder blades
photograph your
asshole you can
photograph mine
make a study for
all the raped and
murdered queers whose
color bled from their wings
push an empty rocking chair
then walk away
make room for
abused spirits
anxious to
get rocking

the wishing
we did at the shopping mall fountain
leveled the place with its own lingering hope
answering the call to arms
with a toy piano
if our cells
have always
been here what
about the rage
what about
depression
marked
with a
story
somewhere
in the world
the jeep that
killed O'Hara
hurts every
time you
start
it

as strong as
our bodies
it is easier to
preserve
the birth
certificate
happy to be
one of two
heartbeats in my bed
maybe I should pay
closer attention
to the lyrics
after sex with
this Nirvana fan
both hands on
his cock
I catch a
glimpse of
mom's urn
wink thank
you for my
wild queer life
learning to linger
over the make them
understand portion of the song

swallowed
each other
until we
heard
each
other
think
queer pirates
I have loved
loosened my
wilderness
no
more
miscounting
butterflies in
our utopia
let's make
poems
that
can
rob
a bank

we wanted this
thing crossing
between us
worming
under
foot a
flavor
revealing
itself to
those who
open the
mouth fully
a taste tasting us back
wide eyed
before we
learn to
catch
words
midair
snorting lines of coke
off the biggest cock
detecting
additional
minutes
hidden in
the cave
we forge
of one
another

it's a commitment
to be the thorns
the rose wears
to the ball
anchored in
the passion
poetry not
proprietary
fancy all you please
but I saw you with
your teeth occupied
tearing flesh from
a leg bone
um resides
between
speaking
thoughts
brittle magic
of the tongue
a picked clean
corpse kind
of day

someone
placed an
anvil in the
sky above
my head
a lucky
fog rolled
over my
enemies
things got better
I leave hair from my
brush on the windowsill
birds weave it into nests
while I sleep I await
their transmissions
a wheel torn from
the rod flying into
another chest
when I wake
sidewalk chalk
ballerina comes
alive in the rain

champions of
not blinking
only the dolls
see it all
our will
to solidify
trumpets
between
strands
of DNA
last time I chose
winter over you
x-ray how wrong
a notion in
my skull
lost in a
pool of
hot wax
beneath
the wick

stretched between
cell phone tower
and the forest
is how I feel
if I do
not touch
the sea
there is
no way
back
grandma
said lucky
was an
option
victory of
water over
knife slicing
the endless
healing surface
please walk with
me to look where
the photographer
pointed the camera
a second
ago

water
from
mouth
of plant
into mine
my parasitic
grip unshaken
a fault following
my own line
a poet with
just enough
dried leaves
to hide phone
car bed
the tv
what's the code
please write it down
got to get it right
required amount
of confidence
to initiate
evolution
of human
branches
leaves
bird
song

mind and
body can only
be separated through
decapitation
another
mistake
we have
lived with
for too long
when it's your
turn go or
hesitate
which
will
it
be
I'm a poet
not a motivational speaker
I keep trying to tell you
press a hand to
the rumbling
wrap yourself in elegy
we kill 3000 silkworms
to make one
pound
of silk

movie of the
memorized
dissolving in
aortic arch of
worms
lovers
wincing
in sunlight
do you own
the land all
the way
to the
core
are
you
a hot
lava
core
owner
barbed wire
and shovel

wagon
full of
could do
would do
america's jaw is
a garbage truck
keep FOR
SALE sign
just in
case
riding
back and
forth on the
violin bow
some
mornings
before waking
the stolen box
of notebooks
vanishes
within
reach

fuck brand loyalty
pull scissors from
the ribbon cutting
ceremony out
of my back
why did you
introduce me
to the man who
invented my
ringtone
now I see him
no matter who calls
this
empire
will
tax
your
soul
I prefer
the forests making
blankets from
themselves

press
accelerator
recalibrated
widow my
period
blood
dream
last night
was purple
smear it on
police station door
Wall Street banker's face
tree surgeon's saw cutting
people to their trunks
prepared to protect
fortunes of ants
say good night
to enemies
with purr
reserved
for lovers

you
were
lonely
before you
started
the war
sound of
a century
diving into
a bucket
we paused
to discuss
how we
almost
died
if we
hold the
near-miss
tighter it
will stop
crying
forever

the american
pork of the
thing kept
coming
at us
I'm sorry
I told him
about the
wasp nest
he heard enlightenment when
I said a new age of entitlement
to scatter his
own ashes he
cremated his
left arm left
leg is next
ears lips
nose
that
is fine
I said
but why
did you
burn the
wasp house
down

never deny
the warmth
of a burning
flag
sing
a 900
year old
death tune
just in time to
digitize empathy
sing it for days
sing it into chairs
sit on it
fold the anus
gingerly around it
hold its sweetest note
till we remember
which ancestor was
the first to forsake
the power
of an
ant

everything
falls with
the tree
something
about the man
in the pin holding
the butterfly down
Dear Reluctant Sleeper
we are supposed to be
used to sleep by now
each night we question
where we are going
why we have to go
our planet much
lighter with
every astronaut
shot into space
jolted alive in the
catapult of ritual
it is a lot of work
but we roll
the world's
barbed wire
into one
ball

woodpeckers
make insects
make themselves
small as possible
marooned in nucleus of
another shattered
discourse your
burning building
appears suddenly
in this poem
a wall
collapses
revealing a line of
detectives waiting
to see if the soul
is betrayed will
we still
believe in
the body
imagine
the body
imagine
us in the
mouselike
dream in
the wall

new crevice
for new
footing
wishes
are all
we work with
never listening
to others
their
worry
piling against
a door they
no longer
see
a
song
to celebrate
being lost
again
today
build
our own
appreciation
for the deer
painted by an
ancient artist

it is easy to
forget there
are other stars
when sunlight
fills me
to the
gills
keeping
a toe in
the dance
music our
preferred
epoxy
I do not
have enough
civic pride for
the grift in
this system
get me out
of the grime of
the sentence
earning love is
like taxing oxygen
how many times are we
asked to overthrow our desire
please say you too are sick of it

without love
nothing would
burden us to
our knees
you are not a
thing I forget is
in my mouth I
promise my man
put my tongue
to his third eye
lick it open
tremble with
baby crow lifted
back into the nest
new miracle
interrupts the
old one long
enough we
reach in
grab
what's needed
Dear Eileen after
a week of
radical honesty
he asked me to lie
I shook my head no
I'm always partly cloudy
he's had plenty of warning

it was
sexy how
you politely
declined the
larger halo
ocean waves travel
thousands of miles
never revealing the
source of their power
enough poems have been
wasted on human cruelty
we dig hard to
find the
other
world
press pen with
everything in us
write Gate to open
9 pages at once
stay open
ignore how much
you want to close
I love you it must
be said I love you
can you hear it arriving
after countless miles
hold my hand as we
feel relief with the
crashing waves

a focus
I mean
a compass
attempting
to understand
our renewal of
winter before we
enter the dance
signing a contract
to control the wind
new arrivals wishing
a ladle of the stuff
on the phone he asks
will you hold me like that again
track ourselves
thru the made
up portion
of a song
we are the
other side of
transmitting
sound into
future warmth
will you do it he asks
I've got the wind I say
with both hands

study how
house is
attached
to planet
to learn
how to
hold on
    slight panic the
        fingerprint
        password
    will not
    remember
grooves in fingers my
mother forged inside
her with a frequency
    that holds the
        shape of
        a leaf
        I was
            born between
            Wooly Bully and
                California Dreamin'
                in the middle of war
                on a military base
                attached to planet
            Earth in Topeka Kansas

without a fortress
everyone must apply
themselves
my dream
president
sleeps in
a tent on
the white
house lawn
lip of earth
lifted for us
to tuck inside
grandma prays
for busy skies of
the rapture
we must
stop flinching
to be held to
be sung to
kneading
songs out
of flesh

the day you see
where you were
not loving
yourself it's
the place they
always find
before
you do
fantasy
of america is
finally too hard
everything they
learned is true
a million
dollars
shoved in
a million
bleeding
mouths
is worth
a million
dollars

one morning
every flying thing
aimed itself at
your pretty
hat
a vowel
the light
unleashed
overhead
we stood
awash with
songs about
time never
holding us
properly
regardless
of suggestion or
complaint carried on a
season of fruit and grain
when love learned to
turn into a sizeable
journey without
leaving the room

redundant as in
quixotic
poet
our
clothes go
up when the sails rip
return to shore
fully exposed
no more
humans
please a
television
show with
a cast of
flowers
aperture
aimed at
lily and
rose
each
dramatic
episode
chrysanthemum
chrysanthemum
my hero my love
chrysanthemum

broken
bowl no
longer a
bowl
apology moonlighting
as compensation
sometimes
gloves get in
the glove box
this is
how
he is
swallowing
everything
worrying
over end
date of
the sky
a good
reaction
when life in
reverse makes
you nauseous

a forgotten
gentleness
we had not
appreciated
enough to
keep it
living
on
our
skin
broken
human
tethering a
soul in place
I wish he would
forgive me but I
know he never will
I said hold yourself
until I get there to
do it for you
hold the stakes
high overhead
higher much
higher we
hope we
can hold
them high
enough

cloud cover with
one orifice one
nomadic
window
riding
the
sky
it
can
take
a very
long time to
return after
being lost
life seems
pliable but
it breaks
keeps
breaking
Smaller
smaller
we cannot glue together
the crumbling glaciers
if we cannot cry it is
possible we are
still lost

losing
something
too important
to lose
is hard
the first
time so
next time
ransom April's song
before it finds itself
I took my time finding
the right man to
build this wall
against the
phantasm
we're rowing to
the middle of
the Bermuda
Triangle we
send our
love

purgatory
is cruel
to poets
a separate
holding tank
where every
melancholy
phrase was
invented
a lifetime
resisting
adjusting
to violence
pity creatures
with the softest fur
the more we dance
the better our poems
trying our best
to cinch it
to hitch it to
the jasmine
ascension

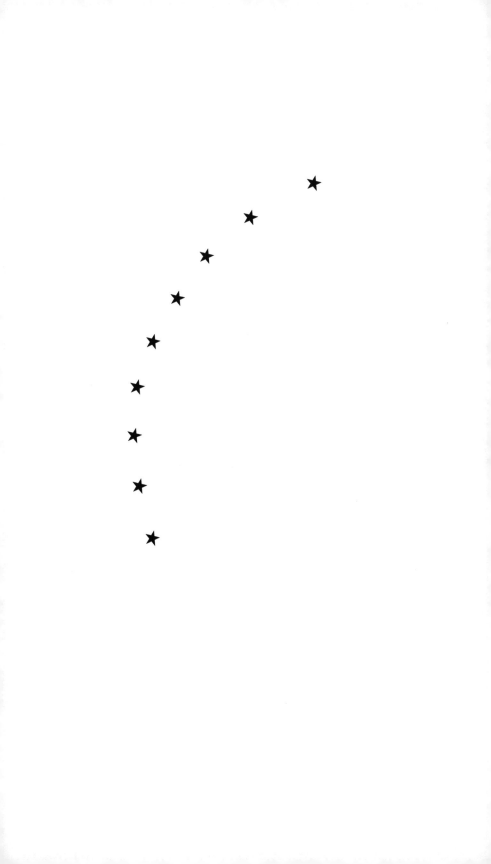

A (Soma)tic Poetry Ritual

The title of this book comes from a poem, and the poem comes from a dream. "I lift / the pen / prepare / for their / answers / when / speaking / with / the / dead / listen to / the golden / boomerang return." The boomerang was flying from my hand, and it spun in place in midair for a long time, turning golden by sunlight that was either sunset or sunrise. While it spun in place, I looked at landmarks to resolve whether the sun was rising or setting. A tree I know well helped me realize the sun was rising, and as soon as I understood this, the boomerang returned to my hand, hot, smooth, and beautiful.

Sunrise made sense because I do most of my writing at dawn when the voices of my dead friends, lovers, and family whisper in my ear to help me make poems. I have determined that they are always there for me, but that I am most relaxed and open in the morning and can distinguish their voices with more accuracy. The boomerang is like the number 7. If we draw 7 from the bottom up in two strokes, it catapults our desires off the tip with force, then arcs to bring them back to us; this is why gamblers love saying "Lucky 7" because it gives them the return of their wishes.

Before writing this book, I associated the origins of boomerangs with the Aboriginal Australian peoples; but they were also in the ancient Americas, India, and Africa. In the pharaoh Tutankhamun's tomb were boomerangs made with beautiful golden tips. It is exciting imagining human beings taking a piece of a tree that grew from the Earth, crafting it with care and attention until the aerodynamics are just right to throw it into the air in front of you and have it ride the invisible currents of oxygen in such a way it can turn around and come home. There are many variations, and not all boomerangs were designed to return, which was also news to me. Weapons, clubs, sports, and musical instruments are some of the many uses of this remarkable ancient tool.

My last collection, *AMANDA PARADISE*, was written while flooding my body with field recordings of recently extinct animals. I wrote the 72 poems in *Listen to the Golden Boomerang Return* with a (Soma)tic poetry ritual which involved writing with fellow animals who have found ways to thrive in the Anthropocene. My need to fall in love again with the world as it is, not as it was, helped me find the ritual for these poems. This new book got its start in Seattle, Washington, during the early days of the Covid-19 pandemic. For the past decade, I have been living on the road, writing while spending time with wildlife in North America.

If you do not know Seattle, it sits inside one of the world's lush and abundant nontropical rainforests and is home to one of the largest populations of crows. They are everywhere in the city, and in their vast numbers, they are unafraid of human beings. Seattle is home to Crow Justice! I watched crows attack a neighbor when he walked to his car because he had taken a broom to them earlier when they gathered on his balcony at sunrise, having their good morning conversation. An orange cat ran in terror from tree to tree to get home, the crows following in the branches above, screaming the alarm.

Each morning when I woke, I would fill a small container on the windowsill with berries, crackers, and peanuts. The crows found them almost immediately, and different groups would visit throughout the day. I ate my meals with them by the window, and one of them in particular liked to eat with me, looking through the window as I smiled and ate my food. Eventually, I could hand this crow food, and I was even allowed to pet their beak. This connection was one of the most beautiful experiences I have ever had with a wild animal. Soon enough, the crow started to bring me gifts.

Gift 1: The crow arrived with a twig. They set it down and tapped their beak on the window. I was always in there; they knew I was not leaving the apartment, hiding from a virus. They shook the twig, set it down, tapped the window, and repeated a couple of times before choosing a cracker and flying away, leaving the twig in the bowl. Honestly, I was not sure if this was a gift. I thought, "Have I been up here alone too long? Did I imagine this?"

Gift 2: After the second gift, there was no doubt this was happening. It is a small piece of translucent plastic, a round, almost glowing nub of a thing. This gift was a decision! They thought, "I know who is going to like this," then brought it to me to thank me or barter with me for nuts and crackers. They were right; I did like it! I do like it! Every time I see it, I fill with joy at the idea that there was care behind it, a thoughtfulness of giving and sharing.

Gift 3: They had a hard time letting go of this red berry, but they wanted me to have it and tapped on the window, leaving it in the bowl for me.

Gifts 4, 5, 6, and 7: These are similar seeds they thought I would enjoy.

Gift 8: When they arrived with this linden tree seed, they twirled and tapped the glass. They expressed so much pleasure in making this seed twirl like a banner.

Gift 9: Seattle sits in the heart of a rainforest made primarily of pine trees. This sliver of pine bark was delicious to smell.

Gift 10: This is a piece of factory-produced dried cat food. They enjoyed eating this brand of food because they would pick it up, wave it, set it down, look at it closely with one eye, then pick it up, set it down, and look at it with the other eye. It was difficult for them to leave behind. I said, "I'm vegan; go ahead and eat it!" But they wanted to share it with me and eventually left it behind.

Gift 11: The day the crow brought this tiny green seed pod was unusually sunny. The natural light made the green seed glow at the tip of their beak as they flew toward me. It felt like the most petite bouquet ever invented, and I loved it!

Gift 12: This is a small, round piece of gold foil, probably a sticker that a teacher puts on a child's homework or exam paper. You need to know that on the night of the first gift, I had a dream that the crow brought me gold. It was long and rectangular gold foil, and a very bossy former boyfriend was in the dream telling me, "That's GOLD! You better thank that crow!" Nothing made me happier than seeing the crow arrive with the gift from my dream!

Each night I broke 9 peanut shells in half when the last group of crows visited before sunset. 9 halves were for the crows; the other 9 were for me. We were asleep with peanuts in our bellies, connecting us across the twinkling lights of downtown. A voice told me in a dream that my poems were now spirits of animals. I saw them moving across the page, looking for something to eat, investigating the edges of the paper where they found themselves trapped.

It was difficult leaving Seattle because this connection was a bond I could feel in my chest as I finally drove away nearly two years after arriving. I received a place to write as part of the Joshua Tree Highlands Artist Residency program, located in the Mojave Desert of California. While there, I used my body to connect with the animals while writing. Artist and curator Eoin Dara wrote to me while I was in Joshua Tree, inviting me to submit a letter for publication in an anthology for the TULCA Festival of Visual Arts in Galway, Ireland. I decided to take the opportunity to write a letter to my boyfriend Tre about the (Soma)tic poetry ritual I was using to make poems at the residency. Here is the letter:

Dearest Tre, it is 45 degrees Celsius this afternoon here in the Mojave Desert. I'm missing you, when do you arrive? The in-

tense heat makes things seem further away; how is it doing that?
Here is a new poem for you. Wet your finger in your mouth and
spell each word onto your chest, and keep that finger moist, my
dear!

losing

something

too important

to lose

is hard

the first

time so

next time

ransom April's song

before it finds itself

I took my time finding

the right man to

build this wall

against the

phantasm

we're rowing to

the middle of

the Bermuda

Triangle we

send our

love

When you get here, I will introduce you to the 9 animals who are
part of my new (Soma)tic poetry ritual. The nocturnal animals
include a band of howling coyotes who comb the sand and cac-
tus around the house each night, looking for something deli-
cious to eat. The kangaroo rat is one of my favorite creatures
who live in this desert. My binoculars are good enough that we
can watch their whiskers and little hands hold sunflower seeds
to nibble while balancing on those massive legs, which actually
evolved to kick their way out of a rattlesnake's jaws! I had a
dream I was breastfeeding a kangaroo rat; it was beautiful! My

mother came in the room and screamed, but you calmed her down while I continued to enjoy feeding my friend whose little claws were gently tangled in my chest hair. "Queers can breastfeed?" I nodded to her, "Yes, I used to breastfeed my stuffed animals as a child, didn't you know?" What a strange thing to dream of my mother seeing me feed a small animal with my body and that you had to intervene on my behalf. Queer needs for queer nerves revealing themselves in new ways.

Remember a few years ago, I asked you to cut my arm with your bowie knife, so I could write a poem while observing my cells in their 27-day repair cycle? There is something special about having the body be part of the writing experience, and with these birds and animals in the desert, each one is assigned a spot on my body. For instance, when the glorious quail come bopping into the yard, running across the sand together, I lightly caress my right jawline with my left thumb. Brush it ever so lightly for 30 seconds. Locating an animal on myself is an incredible way to enter the writing. You will LOVE THIS: the kangaroo rat is my left nipple. After the dream, how could it be any other part of me!? The coyotes are the backs of my ears. I can easily imagine that if one of them let me rub the back of their ears, they would like it a lot!

The lizard gets the spot just below my navel. I have no idea why my dear before you ask! You will have plenty of ideas, but hear me say the body needs our intuitive touch, the imagined cartographies of the flesh! Let's rub our bodies when we see creatures; in fact, let's scratch each other's ears when the coyotes howl! Let's do it! I'm ready! The roadrunner is the most aggressive creature who visits, and I rub my spine, all the way up and down I rub it. Chipmunks are my ankles, and I love how they stretch their bodies on the shaded cement patio to cool their bellies while eating peanuts and cherries. One day the roadrunner tried to catch and eat a chipmunk, and I was grateful for my little furry friend's speed.

Doves are my hands, and I think it is from a television commercial of my childhood about a brand of soap named Dove. It irritates me, but there is nothing I can do about it. If I see doves or even hear them without seeing them, I feel them in my hands. It is not too much to surrender to in the end. And I like the doves and very much enjoy the use of my hands. My gratitude to doves and hands—the perfect time to say I love you! Solar plexus to solar plexus! Your private forest witch, CAConrad

There were many other places where I wrote the poems in this book. There is a busy bridge in Tucson, Arizona, near a grocery store where thousands of bats sleep under the bridge during the day. In the evening, the sky fills with them. One of my favorite living artists, Jason Dodge, invited me to the MACRO in Rome, Italy. I lived inside the museum for a week to spend time with exhibits, including Jason's, which he named after a line in a poem of mine from *AMANDA PARADISE*, "Cut a Door in the Wolf." I would go into the city each morning to watch the sunrise near a fountain. I brought berries and oats to feed rats and pigeons. A beautiful woman would push her gray hair behind an ear and make a chip-chip sound for the rats to appear, and they did! She told me the police would arrest us if they caught us feeding them, so we took turns looking out for one another.

My mother died suddenly and unexpectedly while I was writing this book. It pains me to know that I was getting ready to drive to see

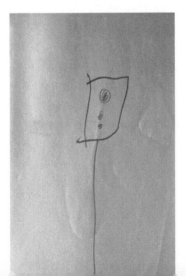

her when I received a call from my cousin Carrie, who put the phone to my mother's ear so she could say goodbye. She saved this drawing in my Baby Book. She told me that when she asked me what it was, I said it was my spirit, my spirit guide, and an enormous scary guardian spirit I could not control flying to planet Earth to get inside her belly and grow my body. The line is the path we took to her from outer space.

In the autumn of 2022, I took a temporary job teaching at the graduate writing program at UMass, Amherst. I found an apartment 27 minutes north in Greenfield, where I signed my first lease in over a decade. I miss being on the road but very much enjoy the extraordinary wildlife of Western Massachusetts. I completed the book while writing with various squirrels, mice, deer, and possums who live in the forest near my new home.

There are 72 poems in total, a number I like very much. There were 73, but I cannibalized one of them, tearing it to pieces to feed to other poems. Mommy has a quota! That is how serious I am about 72. If it comes to 73, someone has to die and live inside the others.

The night after I turned the poems over to my publisher, I dreamt of coming home with bags of groceries to find 6 of the new poems having sex on my bed. They were really going at it, piling on one another. When they saw me, they started throwing letters at me. Their angry voices were growls, yips, and snarls, as though they could not say the words they were made of, and I remember thinking, "Can I teach them to talk?" They were too angry at me for any conversation about learning new things. One of them galloped to the edge of the bed to better aim the letters at my face. I felt the sting again and again.

The following day when I woke, I realized those 6 poems all contained the cannibalized lines from the poem I removed from the manuscript. Were the cannibalized lines forcing the poems to have an orgy to feel reconnected to the whole poem it used to be? Was it a sodomy magic spell I had interrupted? Also, I was coming home with groceries, meaning I was preparing new meals for energy to write new poems now that I had finished the book. What if they were trying to keep themselves alive and were angry at me for abandoning them? These days the poems have more control over me than I do over them, an arrangement I am happy with; I am their devoted servant and would breastfeed them if I could. We take a few years carving these things out of us; then, we give them away just like that. Is it okay if our poems have orgies in our dreams so they can feel alive? I will say yes, it's fine; it is glorious! Let them figure it out their way.

My poems are breathing wild creatures. They stand on the bottom of the page, vibrating in the center of their bodies. If they were to come off the page to live with me, I would work hard to buy a house with many rooms. We would share a large bed; if they learned to jump back on the page when needed, I could take them wherever I went! When my poems become books, I have no control over how other humans feel or think about them, and I'm okay with that so long as I can have my private way of being together with them. If possible, I would like a witness to ensure that there are copies of all my books with me when they put me in the oven to cremate my body. Our ashes need to mix.

Acknowledgments

I am grateful to everyone for taking such excellent care of my poems at Wave Books. So glad and sometimes astonished we are alive to write and read in this violent new age of disease, war, and death.

Many thanks to James Berg and Frederick Fulmer at Joshua Tree Highlands Artist Residency program in Southern California, and to Jason Dodge, Luca Lo Pinto, and the many people at MACRO in Rome, Italy. This book would not exist without their devotion to creating what is necessary for the poems to come to life!

Many thanks to Peter Gizzi. When he offered me the job to fill in for him in the graduate creative writing MFA program at the University of Massachusetts in Amherst, I had been living on the road for over a decade. This opportunity gave me my new home in Greenfield, Massachusetts, where I got to finish this book with the astonishing wild creatures who thrive in the American Northeast.

Finally, but not least, my gratitude to the animals I met. To hear the sniffing, chewing, howling, squeaking, and fluttering, to listen to their breath is to know the sounds that make the world around us whole. We are vibrating across airwaves to connect, and we can understand one another if we take the risk. Rats, for instance, need our love; I insist on it! These creatures so many people despise have flourished despite every attempt we have made to exterminate them from the planet. It is time to stop poisoning, bludgeoning, and murdering creatures who have done nothing wrong but be born. It is time to reconcile our extreme pathology and violence against life that has as much right to be here as we do!

These poems appeared first in magazines and as chapbooks; my thanks to the many editors, publishers, translators, and designers who generously used their efforts and talents to give my poems an audience. I am also very grateful to the curators of the museums and galleries who worked hard to exhibit some of these poems as art objects.

MAGAZINES

032c, About Place, Academy of American Poets, American Poetry Review, The Anarchist Review of Books, Artforum, Art Viewer, The Babel Tower, Blazing Stadium, Bombay Gin, The Brierfield Reader, The Capilano Review, Citrine Pulse, Copenhagen, Cultured, Cunning Folk, Flypaper Lit, Frieze, Green Linden, Hurricane Review, Kyanite, Lakshmi, Looky Here Magazine, Mary Journal, Massachusetts Review, Michigan Quarterly Review, New Republic, The New York Times, Osmosis, Peste Magazine, Pocket Lint, Poetry, The Poetry Review (UK), *Poetry Therapy* (Italy), *The Posthumanist, The Quarterly Review, Stone Pacific Zine, Three Fold, Tribes, A Velvet Giant, Visible Binary, When Is Now,* and *Women's Studies.*

CHAPBOOKS

Listen to the Golden Boomerang Return (H//O//F, 2022)
Poems for Martin, Gunnar, and Martin (GB, 2022)
I Prefer the Forests Making Blankets from Themselves (Bloof Books, 2023)
to desire the world as it is not as it was (Michigan State, 2023)

OTHER BOOKS

Die Sein: Para Psychics, by Kerstin Brätsch (Ludwig Forum Aachen, 2022)
You Don't Have What It Takes to Be My Nemesis, by CAConrad (Penguin UK, 2023)
Negative Space, by A.K. Burns (Dancing Foxes & Wexner Center for the Arts, 2023)

Hidden in the Cave We Forge of One Another, by CAConrad (Cinema Batalha, 2023)

Essential Queer Voices of U.S. Poetry, edited by Christopher Nelson (Green Linden, 2024)

Personal Best: Makers on Their Poems that Matter Most, edited by Erin Belieu and Carl Phillips (Copper Canyon Press, 2023)

there's nothing here but flesh and bone, there's nothing more, edited by Eoin Dara (TULCA Publishing, Galway, 2021)

EXHIBITIONS OF POEMS AS ART OBJECTS

Tai Kwun Contemporary in Hong Kong: *trust & confusion*, curated by Xue Tan and Raimundas Malašauskas, 2021

2021 Riga International Biennial of Contemporary Art, curated by Laima Rudुša

Open Studios in the Netherlands: *Undead Matter*, curated by Sophie Williamson, 2021

Fluent Gallery in Santander, Spain: *13 Moons: Listen to the Golden Boomerang Return*, solo show of poems as art objects, curated by Alex Alonso, 2022

Gropius Bau in Berlin, Germany: SERAFINE1369's *visions*, curated by Zippora Elders, Jennifer Sréter, and Deiara Kouto, 2022

april april Gallery in Brooklyn, New York: Luz Carabaño's *Unfoldings*, curated by Patrick Bova, 2022

Deering Estate, Miami: *Closer to Nature*, curated by Summer Leavitt, 2023

Cinema Batalha in Porto, Portugal: *Hidden in the Cave We Forge of One Another*, solo show of poems as art objects, curated by Alice dos Reis and Isadora Pedro Neves Marques, 2023

OTHER PUBLICATIONS

SOFTSCORES, music by Claire Vivianne Sobottke, Jared Gradinger, and Tian Rotteveel (PACT Zollverein, Essen, 2021)

Ecopoetics Pamphlet, curated by Jonathan Skinner for the COP26 climate negotiations in Glasgow, Scotland

broadside of 3 poems in landscape (GB, 2022)

broadside of 3 poems in landscape (Glasgow University, 2023)

broadside of 3 poems in landscape (Michigan State, 2023)

commissioned by Burg Hülshoff-Center for Literature as part of the project *Masculine Fairies* by Jonas Monka and Minna Wündrich curated by Jenni Bohn

"Twelve Poets," a collaboration with Nicole Eisenman, The Poetry Project, and Hauser & Wirth (*Ursula*, 2023)

CAConrad has worked with the ancient technologies of poetry and ritual since 1975. They are the author of 9 books, including *AMANDA PARADISE: Resurrect Extinct Vibration* (Wave Books, 2021), which won the 2022 PEN Josephine Miles Award. They received a 2022 Ruth Lilly Poetry Prize, a Creative Capital grant, a Pew Fellowship, and a Lambda Award. They exhibit poems as art objects with recent solo shows in Spain and Portugal, and their play *The Obituary Show* was made into a film in 2022 by Augusto Cascales. UK Penguin published two books in 2023. Visit them online at www.linktr.ee/CAConrad88.